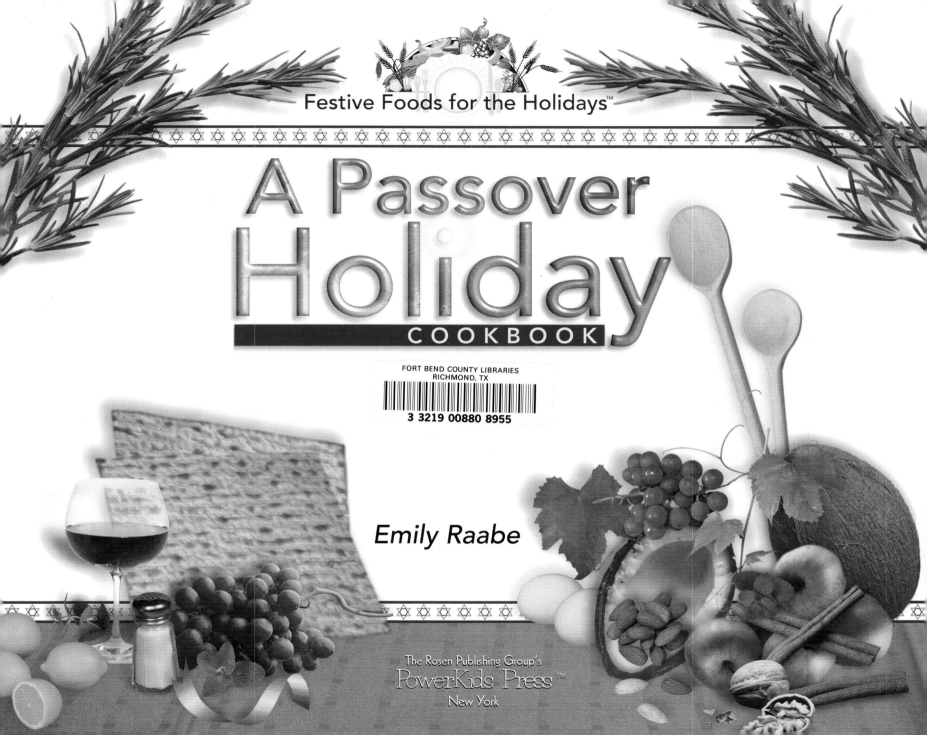

Festive Foods for the Holidays™

A Passover
Holiday
COOKBOOK

Emily Raabe

The Rosen Publishing Group's
PowerKids Press™
New York

The recipes in this cookbook
are intended for a child to make together with an adult.

Many thanks to Ruth Rosen and her test kitchen

For Rachel, my favorite chef

Published in 2002 by The Rosen Publishing Group, Inc.
29 East 21st Street, New York, NY 10010

First Edition

Book Design: Maria E. Melendez

Project Editor: Frances E. Ruffin

Photo Credits: p. 3 © StockFood/Eising; p. 4 © Bettmann/CORBIS; p. 7 © Jewish Museum, New York/SuperStock; p. 8 © Bibliotheque Nationale, Paris/SuperStock; p. 14 © SuperStock; p. 17 (Apples) © StockFood/Eising; p. 17 (Walnuts) © StockFood America/Schieren; p. 18 © Patrick Ramsey/International Stock.

Raabe, Emily.
    A Passover holiday cookbook / Emily Raabe.
       p. cm.— (Festive foods for the holidays)
    ISBN 0-8239-5625-3
    1. Passover cookery—Juvenile literature. [1. Passover. 2. Passover cookery. 3. Holidays. 4. Cookery, International.] I. Title. II. Series.
       TX739.2.P37 R33 2002
       641.5'676—dc21   00-012443

Manufactured in the United States of America

Contents

The Story of Passover

Jewish people celebrate Passover every year at the beginning of spring. Passover always falls on the 15th day of the month of Nissan in the Jewish **lunar calendar**. In our modern calendar, this holiday is close to Easter. During Passover, Jewish people remember the amazing story of how their **ancestors** escaped from **slavery** in Egypt about 3,000 years ago. The Passover holiday lasts for eight days and nights. In the country of Israel, Passover lasts for seven days and nights. Food, stories, and sharing memories are at the center of the Passover celebration. The foods served and eaten during this holiday are reminders of events in Jewish history.

Passover is a time to celebrate with family and friends.

5

Escape from Egypt

About 3,000 years ago, the Jewish people were called the Israelites. A man named Pharaoh, who ruled Egypt, **enslaved** the Israelites. Jewish legend says God spoke to a Jewish **shepherd** named Moses. God told Moses to ask Pharaoh to set the Jewish people free. Moses did this, but Pharaoh refused to free the Jewish people. According to the Bible, God then punished the Egyptian people with terrible **plagues**. The stories say that God made cattle sick, turned rivers into blood, made the daytime turn dark, and had the Egyptians suffer. Still, Pharaoh would not let the Israelites go free.

According to a Bible story, God appeared in the form of a burning bush and spoke to Moses.

6

Passing Over

The Hebrew name for Passover is Pesach, meaning "passing over." The Israelites spoke Hebrew. This language is still spoken by Jews in Israel today. Jewish legend says the last plague that God sent down was to have an angel kill all of the Egyptians' firstborn sons. God instructed Moses to tell the Jews to mark their houses so that the angel of God would "pass over" them and leave the Jewish sons in safety. Egypt's Pharaoh finally gave in and set the Jewish slaves free. Then he changed his mind and sent his armies after the Jews. God helped Moses split the Red Sea, which lay between Egypt and Israel. This made a dry path for the Israelites to pass through in safety.

When Pharaoh's armies tried to follow the Israelites, God closed the sea against them, and Pharaoh's armies were drowned. The Israelites were set free. Passover is a celebration of this freedom.

9

Matzo

The Israelites had to leave Egypt quickly. They left so quickly that they had no time to wait for their bread dough to rise. Instead they had to dry the dough in the hot desert sun. The sun dried the dough into thin, flat bread that was like a cracker. Today, when Jewish people celebrate Passover, they eat a food called matzo. Matzo is bread that has no yeast in it. Yeast is what makes bread dough rise. Because it has no yeast in it, matzo is thin and hard, like a cracker. Jewish people eat matzo during Passover. That helps them remember that when their ancestors fled Egypt, they did not have time to wait for their bread dough to rise. One way to eat matzo is to mix it with eggs and fry it like a pancake. This is called matzo brie.

10

Matzo Brie

You will need:

2 eggs

¼ teaspoon (1.2 ml) salt

2 teaspoons (9.9 ml) grated onion (have an adult help you grate the onion)

2 sheets matzos (find matzos in supermarket ethnic food sections)

2 teaspoons (9.9 ml) vegetable oil

How to do it:

Stir the eggs with a fork in a small bowl.

Add salt and grated onion.

Soak the matzos under the faucet in warm water for a few seconds.

Crumble them into the eggs, leaving pieces coarse. Mix well.

Have an adult help you heat vegetable oil in a small, heavy frying pan.

Pour in egg-matzo mixture.

Let the matzo brie brown on one side, turn it over with a spatula and let the second side brown.

Serve matzo brie hot with pancake syrup, strawberry jam, or honey.

This recipe serves two people.

Chametz

Just before Passover, every Jewish home is cleaned from top to bottom. This is done to get rid of every last crumb of bread and food that has yeast in it. Jewish people call these forbidden foods chametz. All the chametz has to be eaten or given away before the holiday starts. Jewish families even use different dishes and silverware during Passover. They want to make sure that they do not touch even a trace of chametz during the holiday. During Passover, food is cooked without using leavening ingredients, such as yeast or baking powder. Instead, Passover foods have matzo meal, which is like cornmeal but made from matzo. Although certain foods are forbidden during Passover, people who keep **kosher** for Passover still can eat many delicious foods that are kosher for Passover, such as chocolate macaroons.

Chocolate Macaroons

You will need:

5½ cups (1.3 l) coconut flakes

14-ounce (.4 l) can of sweetened condensed milk

3 tablespoons (44 ml) unsweetened cocoa

2 teaspoons (9.9 ml) vanilla extract

1½ teaspoons (7.4 ml) almond extract

How to do it:

Have an adult help you set the oven at 350 degrees Fahrenheit (177 degrees C).

Combine all ingredients in a large bowl.

Mix well.

Using a teaspoon, drop the dough onto a foil-lined, well-oiled cookie sheet.

Bake 10 minutes or until the edges are crisp and brown.

Remove from cookie sheet immediately.

Cool on a wire rack.

The Seder Meals

The first two nights of Passover are celebrated with special dinners called **seders**. In Israel, because the Passover holiday lasts for only seven days, the seder is for one night. The first seder meal begins after sundown on the first day of Passover. During seder meals, Jewish families pray, sing, and retell the story of the Israelites' escape from Egypt. Children at the seder meals take part in the storytelling. They also can help to prepare the special foods for Passover. Grandparents and parents share Passover recipes with their children. Although the seder is serious, it is also a joyful celebration and a time to relax with friends and family.

The seder plate is divided into several sections. The food in each section represents the Jewish people's escape from Egypt.

15

The Seder Plate

In the center of the seder table is the seder plate. This plate is divided into sections and has different foods in each section. Each food **represents** certain things from the story of the Jewish people's escape from Egypt. The foods on the seder plate are charoset, parsley, roasted egg, a roasted lamb bone, and bitter herbs. Charoset, an apple mixture, represents the **mortar**, or cement, that the Jewish slaves used to make bricks for Pharaoh. Parsley represents springtime and hope. Dipped into saltwater, it represents the tears of the Jewish slaves. The egg is a **symbol** of spring, when new things are born. The lamb bone represents the animal **sacrifice** that the Israelites made to God when they became free. Bitter herbs, such as horseradish, represent the sadness of slavery.

Charoset

You will need:

2 grated apples
Juice of one lemon
1 cup (23 cl) finely
    chopped walnuts
1 tablespoon (14.8 ml)
    grape juice
1½ teaspoons
    (7.4 ml) sugar

How to do it:

Wash and peel the apples.

Remove apple cores. Have an adult help you to
    grate the apples into a bowl.

Sprinkle grated apple with lemon juice.

Add chopped walnuts.

Stir in the grape juice.

Sprinkle the top with sugar.

Serve on the seder plate.

Welcoming Elijah

During the Passover seder, people drink wine or grape juice. They refill their glasses four times. These four glasses of wine are symbols of the different stages of the Israelites' escape to freedom. Another glass of wine is filled and put on the table for the **prophet** Elijah, the Jewish **savior**. Jews believe that Elijah visits every Jewish home on Passover.

Another seder tradition is to place three pieces of matzo under a cloth cover on the seder table. One piece of matzo is broken in half. One half of the broken matzo is put back under the napkin, and the other half is hidden for children to find after the meal. Sometimes the lucky child who finds this hidden piece receives a prize.

During the seder, a family member, usually the youngest, opens the door to welcome Elijah into their home.

19

Passover
Around the World

Jewish people around the world celebrate Passover. Although the celebration is usually the same no matter where you live, the food can be slightly different. In the United States, the charoset is made of apples, walnuts, and sweet wine. In Italy, Jewish families make their charoset from dates, oranges, raisins, and figs. In some countries in Africa, the main part of the seder meal might be a rice and vegetable dish. In France, Germany, and elsewhere, rice is a food that is not eaten at all during Passover. Families in America often start the seder meal with gefilte fish and matzo ball soup. For the main part of the dinner, they might have beef or roast turkey. A popular dish in both America and Israel is sweet potato kugel. This dish can be a main dish or a sweet dessert.

20

Sweet Potato Kugel

You will need:

6 small sweet
    potatoes
3 apples
1 cup (23 cl) raisins
1 cup (23 cl) matzo
    meal
2 teaspoons (11.8 ml)
    cinnamon
1 cup (23 cl)
    chopped walnuts
1 cup (23 cl) fruit
    juice or water

How to do it:

Have an adult heat the oven to 375 degrees Fahrenheit
    (191 degrees C).

Wash and peel the sweet potatoes and apples.

Remove apple cores.

Have an adult help you to grate the apples and sweet
    potatoes into a bowl.

Mix all ingredients together in a large bowl.

Pour mixture into a well-greased baking dish.

Bake uncovered for 45 minutes or until crisp on top.

This recipe serves 10 to 12 as a side dish for a
    Passover dinner.

Passover Is Celebration

Passover is sometimes called The Spring Festival. The joyful celebration of Passover welcomes the end of winter and the beginning of spring. It is also sometimes called The Time of Our Freedom. It helps people to remember the sadness of slavery, and then the joy that the Israelites felt when they were freed from their long slavery. Certain foods cannot be eaten during Passover, but there are many delicious foods that are eaten especially at Passover. Learning to make some of those foods can be a great way to keep alive the **traditions** surrounding the holiday. No matter where in the world the Passover holiday is celebrated, it is always a wonderful time to cook, eat, remember the past, and to celebrate with family and friends.

22

Glossary

enslaved (in-SLAYVD) To have taken away a person's freedom.

kosher (KOH-shur) Food prepared according to Jewish law.

lunar calendar (LOO-nur KAH-len-dur) A calendar that is based on the cycles of the moon.

mortar (MOR-tur) Matter that is used to harden building materials.

plagues (PLAYGZ) Very dangerous diseases, curses, or hardships.

prophet (PRAH-fet) A religious leader who speaks as the voice of God.

represents (reh-prih-ZENTS) Stands for.

sacrifice (SA-krih-fys) To give up something for an ideal or a belief.

savior (SAYV-yur) A person who saves or rescues.

seders (SAY-durz) Celebrations and dinners during the first two days of Passover. In Hebrew, seder means order.

shepherd (SHEH-perd) The person who cares for and herds sheep.

slavery (SLAY-ver-ee) The system of one person "owning" another.

symbol (SIM-bul) An object that stands for something important.

traditions (truh-DIH-shunz) Ways of doing something that get passed down through the years.

23

Index

Web Sites

To learn more about Passover, check out these Web sites:
www.holidays.net/Passover/
www.kidsdomain.com/holiday/passover/

24